The Ancient
GREEKS

Revised and Updated

PAT TAYLOR

Heinemann Library
Chicago, Illinois

© 1998, 2007 Heinemann Library
a division of Reed Elsevier Inc.
Chicago, Illinois

Customer Service 888-454-2279
Visit our website at www.heinemannraintree.com

Designed by Richard Parker and Q2A Solutions
Printed in China by WKT Company Ltd

11 10 09 08 07
10 9 8 7 6 5 4 3 2 1

New edition ISBNs:
1-403-48811-8 (hardback)
1-403-48818-5 (paperback)

13 digit ISBNs:
978-1-403-48811-4 (hardback)
978-1-403-48818-3 (paperback)

The Library of Congress has cataloged the first edition of this book as follows:
Taylor, Pat, 1948-
  The ancient Greeks / Pat Taylor.
  p.   cm. — (History opens windows)
  Includes index.
  Summary: An introduction to various elements of ancient Greek civilization including gods and goddesses, clothing, food, town and country life, art and theater, and the Olympic games.
  ISBN 0-431-05704-4 (lib. bind.)
  1. Greece—Civilization—To 146 B.C.—Juvenile literature.
  [1. Greece—Civilization—To 146 B.C.] I. Title. II. Series.
  DF77.T35   1997
  938—DC21
                        96-53223
                        CIP
                        AC

Acknowledgments
The publishers would like to thank the following for permission to reproduce photographs:
Alamy, p. **27**; Photographers' Library, p. **7**; Michael Holford, pp. **9**, **15**; H. L. Pierce Fund, Museum of Fine Arts, Boston, p. **10**; Sonia Halliday Photographs, pp. **22**, **25**; Ancient Art and Architecture Collection/Ronald Sheridan, pp. **24**, **29**.

Cover photograph reproduced with permission of The Art Archive / Archeological Museum Naples / Dagli Orti.

Contents

Some words are shown in bold, **like this**.
You can find out what they mean by looking in the glossary.

Introduction

Greece is a rocky country. Many of its people live near the sea. There are many islands.

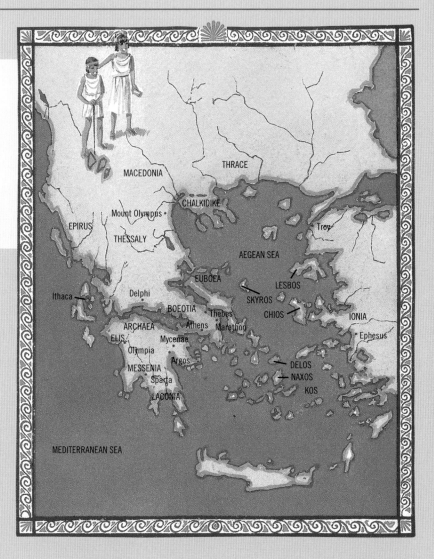

MACEDONIA

THRACE

CHALKIDIKE

Mount Olympus

EPIRUS

THESSALY

Troy

AEGEAN SEA

EUBOEA

LESBOS

SKYROS

Delphi

Ithaca

BOEOTIA

Thebes

CHIOS

IONIA

ARCHAEA

Athens

Marathon

Ephesus

ELIS

Mycenae

Olympia

DELOS

MESSENIA

Argos

NAXOS

Sparta

KOS

LACONIA

MEDITERRANEAN SEA

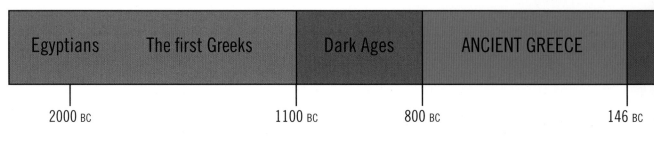

356–323 BC: Alexander the Great

Egyptians	The first Greeks	Dark Ages	ANCIENT GREECE

2000 BC   1100 BC   800 BC   146 BC

People lived in Greece from the earliest times. Different groups of people organized their lives in different ways. They did not think of themselves as Greeks. By 800 BC, villages began to grow into towns. Some of the Greeks made **city-states**. They traded with each other and with other countries. Some of the city-states such as Athens became very rich. Much of the evidence we have from ancient Greece is from Athens. The people made beautiful vase paintings and statues. They wrote stories, poems, and plays. They knew about science and math. We still use many of their ideas. Some of the letters of our alphabet come from Greek letters.

Sometimes the city-states fought each other. Sometimes they fought together against other countries. In 499 BC they started to fight against Persia. Alexander the Great ruled all of Greece, but when he died his land was split up. The **Romans** took control of Greece in 146 BC. You can see this marked on the timeline below.

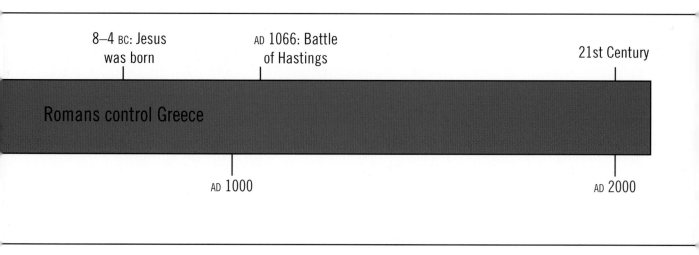

8–4 BC: Jesus was born

AD 1066: Battle of Hastings

21st Century

Romans control Greece

AD 1000

AD 2000

Gods and Goddesses

The Greeks believed in many gods and goddesses. They believed that the gods controlled everything, from the weather to the way people felt. People believed that some of the gods and goddesses lived on Mount Olympus. There are many stories about Greek gods and goddesses that we can read today.

Hermes
Messenger of the gods.

Zeus
The most important god.

Hera
Wife of Zeus and queen of heaven.

These are some of the Greek gods and goddesses.

Athena
Goddess of wisdom.

Apollo
God of music. People went to his temple if they wanted to know about the future.

The Greeks built **temples** in every town. Each one was for a particular god or goddess. People went to the temples to pray. Sometimes they took a gift. If this was an animal the priest would **sacrifice** it. They cooked the meat and ate it. They burned the bones and fat as an offering for the god.

The Parthenon is an ancient Greek temple in Athens. It was built for the goddess Athena.

This is the Parthenon. It had an enormous statue of Athena in it.

Clothes

Greek people wore loose clothes because Greece is hot in summer. We can tell what they wore from their vase paintings and statues. Most people wore a **tunic** called a chiton. It was made from two rectangular pieces of cloth with holes for the head and arms. Girls and boys dressed alike in short chitons. Men and women wore long ones. In winter they wore a cloak called a himation.

This is a Greek family with their slaves.

The Greek woman sitting down is having a necklace put on her. This scene is from a vase painting.

Rich people's clothes were made of wool or linen. Sometimes their clothes were brightly colored. They wore boots or sandals. The women wore makeup. On special occasions women may have worn fine wigs.

Poor people and **slaves** did not wear shoes. Their clothes were usually made from wool.

Food

The Greeks ate a variety of foods. They enjoyed a lot of fish. They only had big pieces of meat at **festivals**. More often they ate small birds such as thrushes and swallows. In addition to meats, the Greeks had lentils, radishes, celery, and beans. They ate cheese, cakes, and fruit. The women, or their **slaves**, ground grain to make flour and bread. They made wine from grapes.

Many Greeks lived by the sea and caught fish to eat. We can see from this vase painting that they used a rod and line. They also used pots to catch lobsters.

Men and women did not eat meals together. The men lay on couches and were given the food by slaves. They had plates made from pottery. They ate with a metal spoon and knife or with their fingers. There was often music and dancing after the meal. Women and children usually ate together.

These men are enjoying a dinner party.

Children

In most parts of ancient Greece, boys were seen as more important than girls. Boys whose families could afford it started school when they were six. They learned to read, write, and add. They also learned to appreciate poetry and music.

The girls helped their mothers around the house. They would cook, weave, and clean. Some were taught to read and write by their mothers. In Sparta, girls went to school and learned to be fit and strong.

This boy is learning how to write.

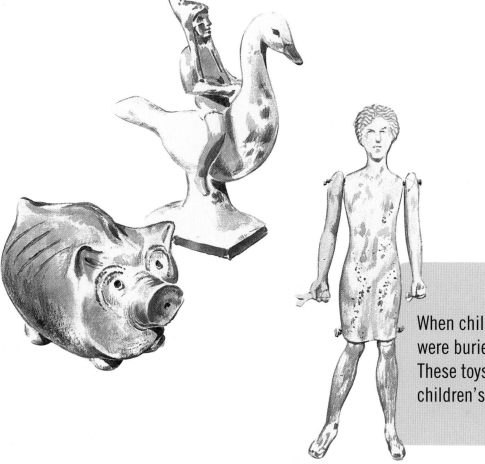

When children died they were buried with their toys. These toys were found in children's graves.

Greek children played with toys that were made of clay or leather.

When they turned 15, Greek girls threw away their toys and married men chosen by their fathers.

When they turned 16, Athenian boys trained for jobs, perhaps as craftworkers. At age 18 they became citizens and could vote. Slaves and women, however, were not allowed to vote.

Health and Sickness

This person is sleeping near the temple of Asclepius to try to get better.

The ancient Greeks tried to stay healthy. They believed that the gods made them ill. If they became ill they went to sleep near the **temple** of the god Asclepius. They thought that this would make them better. They also made medicine from plants.

These are tools that Greek doctors used. The cup was used to catch blood. The knife was used to cut off legs and arms. The tweezers were used to pull out spearheads. The spoon was for giving medicine.

Greek doctors had new ideas about why a person became ill. The most famous of these doctors was Hippocrates. He did not think that illness came from the gods. Some of his ideas about how a doctor should work are still in use today.

Buildings

Some Greek buildings still stand today. These were the important buildings such as **temples** and theaters. Many of them took years to build. Stones had to be carried on wagons from the quarries. They were lifted by ropes and pulleys and held together with pieces of wood and metal.

Many Greek buildings had columns to hold up their roofs. There are three styles of columns: Doric, Ionic, and Corinthian.

Houses were made of mud bricks. They were not built to last. Poor people's houses were very simple. Rich people's houses had large, cool rooms, built around a courtyard. Women lived in a separate part of the house.

There was not much furniture in Greek houses.

The first columns that the Greeks built were plain. Later the columns were more decorated.

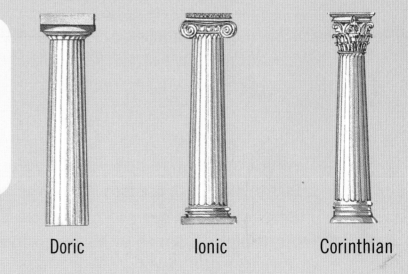

Doric   Ionic   Corinthian

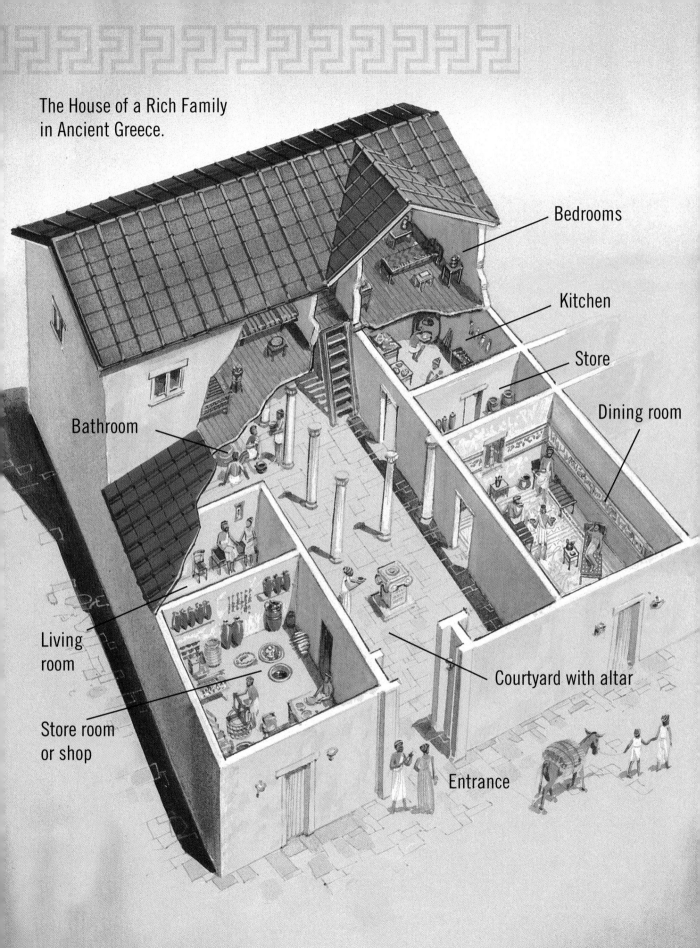

The House of a Rich Family in Ancient Greece.

Bedrooms

Kitchen

Store

Dining room

Bathroom

Living room

Store room or shop

Courtyard with altar

Entrance

Town Life

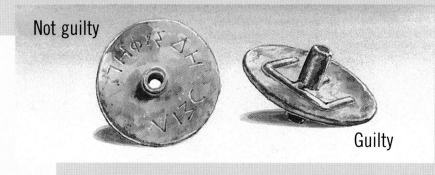

Not guilty

Guilty

These disks were used in the law courts. They would announce if a person was guilty or not guilty.

Ancient Greece was divided into small areas called **city-states**. Athens and Sparta were the only big towns. Each city-state had its own laws. Sometimes it had its own coins and army. At its center was a town with a fortified hill called an acropolis.

Athens was a democracy. This means that every man born in Athens, unless he was a **slave**, could vote on how the city-state was run.

In the middle of the town was the **agora**. This is where the main buildings were. It was also a meeting place. There were bankers' stalls, market stalls, law courts, and **slave-dealers**. People would walk around and chat. There were acrobats and musicians. Around the agora were the town houses. Craftworkers lived in these houses. The fronts of their houses were their workshops.

The agora was a very busy place in a Greek town.

Trade and Ships

The ancient Greeks traded with other countries such as Egypt, Syria, and Sicily. The Greeks found it easier to travel by sea than over land because of the mountains and poor roads. The Greeks figured out where they were going by looking at the stars. They built **merchant ships** to carry their goods. The ships carried **slaves**, wood, corn, iron, and copper.

Leather ropes

Linen sail

At first the Greeks bartered (swapped) their goods. Later, some **city-states** had their own coins. This is the owl of Athens.

Hull

Bow

Ram

The merchant ships were made of wood and had a large hold to carry the **cargo**. They had a sail and many oars. They were slow and heavy, but there were other Greek ships that were lighter. These were warships called triremes, like the one in the picture. In peacetime they could protect the merchant ships from pirates. They had a ram to hit other ships. They had three rows of oarsmen and could carry 200 men.

Stern

Steering oar

Painted eye to keep evil spirits away or for the ship to see where it was going

Country Life

Most Greek people lived in the country and were farmers. It was a hard life. The soil was rocky and did not grow very good crops. It rained a lot in the winter and very little in the summer. The summer was also very hot.

Grapes grew on the sides of the hills. Olive trees grew on the poor soil, just as they do today. On the better soil, the Greeks grew corn. They also raised donkeys, sheep, and goats.

This is what Greece looks like now. It has not changed much since the time of the ancient Greeks. It is a hot, dry, and rocky place.

This picture shows people at work in the country. Women and children did their share of the work.

The roads were very poor and hilly, and most people walked. Some people had horses and carts. Rich people rode horses. Craftworkers made and mended carts and tools. There were herders to take care of the animals. There were also miners who dug for silver.

The Olympic Games

The Greeks liked sports. Many believe that the Olympic Games began in 776 BC. They were held in the city of Olympia every four years.

The Games started with a **sacrifice** to Zeus. Some events, such as **chariot** racing, are not in the Games we have today. Other events, such as the pentathlon, still are. To win the pentathlon, athletes had to complete five events: discus throwing, javelin throwing, wrestling, running, and long jumping. Winners of all races were given wreaths of olive leaves to wear on their heads.

This is a famous statue of a discus thrower. A Greek discus was a flat metal plate.

This is a Greek stadium. The athletes ran one or two stades. A stade was about 650 feet (200 meters). The spectators sat on the stone seats.

Olympia had a **stadium**, **baths**, and **temples**. We can still see the remains of some of these buildings.

The Olympic Games were stopped by the **emperor** Theodosius in AD 393. Then, in 1896, they were started again. Today there are Winter and Summer Games, held every four years. The Games begin when an athlete lights a special flame with a torch brought from Olympia.

Art and Theater

The ancient Greeks enjoyed many types of art. They liked paintings, music, poems, and statues. They told many stories about their gods and heroes. Their painted vases tell us what they did and what they looked like. The statues were usually painted, though the paint has worn off now. We do not know what their music sounded like.

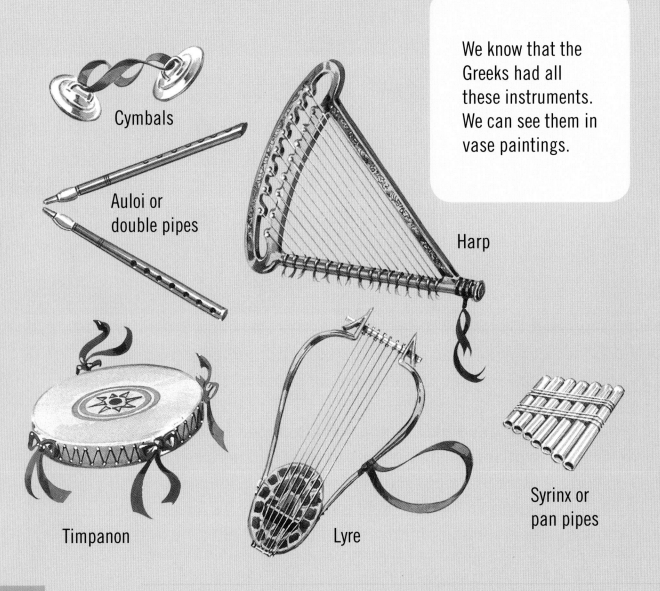

We know that the Greeks had all these instruments. We can see them in vase paintings.

Cymbals

Auloi or double pipes

Harp

Timpanon

Lyre

Syrinx or pan pipes

Many Greek towns had an open-air theater. These theaters were only used for **festivals**. People watched about four plays, one after the other. The plays were either funny (comedies) or sad (tragedies). All the actors were men. They had to play more than one part. They wore masks to show which parts they were playing.

Greek plays are still performed today. This one is in an ancient Greek theater.

Great Thinkers

The Greeks wanted to know about their world. Was the Earth flat? What happened to the Sun at night? Where were the stars in the daytime? They would sit in the **agora** and talk, telling each other their ideas. They wanted to know about many things, such as water. A famous thinker named Archimedes discovered how to move water uphill.

This is the screw that Archimedes invented to carry water uphill.

Plato

Socrates

Herodotus

These are statues of famous Greeks.

Some Greeks, such as Pythagoras, studied math and looked at shapes and angles. Some, like Socrates, wondered what made people behave the way they did. Some thought about good and evil. Some, such as Plato, thought about how countries should be ruled. Herodotus wrote history books. His books tell us about the Greeks and other people.

Alexander the Great

We know a lot about the ancient Greek ruler Alexander the Great. He was taught by Aristotle, an important thinker. Alexander the Great ruled Greece after his father Philip died. He won many battles and took over many lands. He later ruled Egypt and built a large city called Alexandria. After he died, all his land was split up. It was later taken by the **Romans**.

This is a picture of Alexander the Great. It was made out of small pieces of colored tiles. It is called a mosaic.

Glossary

agora busy central area in ancient Greek cities, where people came together

baths public bath house, with pools for relaxing and swimming in

cargo goods carried on a ship

chariot small, horse-drawn vehicle

city-state city that became powerful and formed its own state, with its own government

emperor ruler who has total power, like a king

festival time of celebration with special events and entertainment

merchant ships ships that carry items that are going to be sold

Romans people of the ancient Roman Empire (500 BC–AD 476)

sacrifice to kill an animal as an offering (gift) to a god or goddess

slave person who belongs to someone else and can be bought and sold

slave-dealer someone who makes a living selling slaves

stadium large sports ground surrounded by rows of seats where people watch the games

temple building for religious worship

tunic garment shaped like a knee-length T-shirt

Find Out More

Books to read

Owens, Greg. *History and Activities of Ancient Greece: Hands on Ancient History.* Chicago: Heinemann Library, 2006.

Shuter, Jane. *Life in Ancient Athens: Picture the Past.* Chicago: Heinemann Library, 2005.

Using the Internet

Explore the Internet to find out more about the ancient Greeks. Use a search engine, such as www.yahooligans.com or www.internet4kids.com and type in a keyword or phrase such as "Parthenon" or "ancient Olympics."

Index